For You

Cover design by Stella Mongodi
Editorial services by Sage Taylor Kingsley
www.SageforYourPage.com

Hardcover ISBN 979-8-9881932-0-3
Paperback ISBN 979-8-9881932-1-0

First Edition

Published by Kavalya Press

kavalyashakti@gmail.com

swava stengel

LETTING IT ALL GO

a collection of poetry

TABLE OF CONTENTS

*The fire of Love blazed in my heart
and consumed everything.
My books, my erudition and my mind
I put away on a shelf.
Now I only write poems.*

-Rumi

There Is a Poetry in My Soul

there is a poetry
in my soul
written on
the parchment
of my pulsing heart

a poem
for each person
my mother
my father
my sister
my brother
my lover
and for every stranger, too

a poem
for every creature
every plant
every flower
the sky
the oceans
the land
the moon
and for the sun, too

for every molecule
that makes up this world

every syllable pregnant
with love
ready to be birthed

a living poem
for God

and yet
it is a poetry
with no words
in a language
not yet invented

please forgive
this strained endeavor
for there is no word yet
that could convey
the poetry of my soul
the love I bear *you*

Who I Am on an Island

the woman who walked a thousand miles
to sit on the shore of her own tears
for two thousand years

until she cried a deluge that left her
an empty and ever-so-still vessel

cross-legged in the sand
waves lapping at the fringes of her skirts

eyes closed
hands folded
head tilted toward the skies

the winds came
and lifted the grains of sand
every one of which was a sadness
she felt piercingly

they swirled around her for millennia
until she was a flesh statue of stone
enclosed in her sorrows
beads of sand
crystallized in salt water

clinging to every wild tendril
of her long-forgotten hair
whipping in the breeze

the sun came and melted her pain
and she turned bronze and glowing

she opened her eyes

centuries had passed

and she quietly and bravely
stood up to return to the world

expanded beyond grief
and intent now
only
on
love

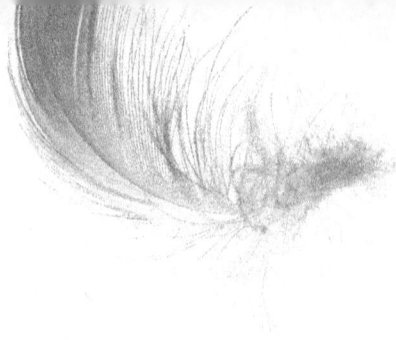

This Holy Now Wow Sacred Moment

wherever you are
stop!

look around you

it's happening:
your life!

with every beat of your heart

with every breath of your soul:
a gift!

this holy now wow sacred moment

don't miss it!

it's *your* precious life

It's Too Late for Me

It's too late for me

I have seen *you*.

In *all* your exquisiteness.

(Nothing is hidden from me.)

And I am in
                    ecstasy.

Your very existence
your tiniest details
bring me to my knees
throw my arms wide open
to embrace everything.

You cannot veil your divinity
or erase what I have seen.

Stay away if you must.
It doesn't matter.
Your radiance will cross oceans
will warm me from wherever you are.

I will worship you from afar.
There is no separating us.
There is no turning back.

Pretend if you must.
I understand
you may like this game
of hide and seek
we invented long ago
but I'm done.

I surrender.

In fact, I've won
because through you
I have become *love*.

I cannot unsee you
in everyone.
In every moment of creation
you are with me.

It can be no other way.

Save yourself if you must
but it's too late for me.

Please Get Wild with Me!

please get wild with me!
let's really *really* let it all go
take off our clothes
dance like maniacs
under the blazing sun

aren't you ready yet
to celebrate
this creation
this grandeur
this *love*?!

let's stop pretending
that we are not in *awe*!
let's finally admit
what we all know

let's stand up on tables!
bring traffic to a halt!
I'll count to three
and we'll yell it together
this huge secret:
"there's only *love*!"

please get wild with me
because I don't think
I can hold it in anymore

this love is seeping
from my pores

grab my hand
run with me
up the tallest mountain

let's spread our wings!
let's fly, my love!

please get wild with me!
let's let it *all* go!

It Goes on While We Sleep

every night I wrap myself
in a blanket of love and gratitude
and I fall asleep
to go meet with you

and all night
we sit by the fire
remembering who we are
singing our ancient songs
drumming and dancing beneath the moon

until dawn calls us back to the world

Let's Not Overcomplicate Things

let's not overcomplicate things
the rules are simple here:

open your heart

love as much as you can

open your heart some more

love even more

expand

and repeat

until your whole being
is flooded with gratitude
and light

and you remember
there's no other way
it can be

Don't Come if You're Not Gonna Dance

there's a big party going on
we're all gonna get *very* crazy
we're celebrating
because we're *free*

we're gonna
stomp our feet!
clap our hands!
throw back our heads!
laugh, shout, sing!
things are gonna get messy

everyone's invited!
but don't come
if you're not gonna dance
this wild time is not for wallflowers
it's not for the timid or afraid
it's for those ready to cast aside
their self-imposed chains
it's for those who are ready
to get really weird

we're calling all freaks
the stranger the better

to really cut loose
to really let it *all* go

so please

don't come
if you're not gonna dance

Shapeshifter

My Beloved is a shapeshifter
playing hide and seek,
always whispering,
"Can you spot me?"

And since *Love* removed the veil
from my once-unseeing eyes,
I have become a master
at seeing him everywhere he hides.

I sense him in the wind
dancing on my skin.
I see him in the vastness
of blue skies
but he's also there
in every single cloud.
I recognize him
in the falling rain
and in the mountains
I pass by.

I catch him in every bird that sings
and riding on butterfly wings.
He's there

in a spider's web
a cat's purr
a frog's croak
a coyote's howl.
He's there
in all laughter.

I feel him in the ocean waves
pulling and pushing me
to come dive in.
I smile when he glides
into my kitchen
on a sunlight beam
and I wink back at him
when he pretends he is the stars.
He is the smell of sage
on my morning hike
and the scent of lavender
in my shower.

He is the tree
I rest my back against.
He is the earth
beneath my feet.
He comes to me
in every stranger's smile
and in my cup of tea.

He is in all the poetry I read
in every word of wisdom given me
in the beat of my heart
in the blood in my veins
in the life
I breathe in
and the love
I exhale.

He is the mirror
reflecting my own face.

There's nowhere
he can hide
from me.

But my favorite place
for us to meet
is when he strides
right up to me
and thinks I won't see,
thinks he's got me
fooled,
when he's pretending
to be
you.

Quantum Entanglement

I lie back

let the stars
come down to me

I float

into the cosmos

held
by infinite glittering limbs
embracing me
loving me

and yet I remain
on Earth
with my Mother

held
by her magnetic pull

I am there
I am here
I am everywhere

and everything is me

my cells vibrate
with the light of Suns
we cannot see

life's energy
flows through me
a river
healing me

anchored I fly

alone yet connected
in form yet formless
separate yet one

I lie back

I expand

and I

breathe

I Am the Calm and Peaceful Lake

look deep inside yourself

past the stormy and rough seas
past the craggy mountains
where thunder and lightning
never allow you peace

past the seemingly eternal barren deserts
past the dark forests of tangled trees

there you'll come upon me
a calm and peaceful lake

sit down upon my shores
lay your burdens at my feet
wipe your tears with my skirts
cry your troubles into my arms

let it all out
your anger
your rage
your sadness
your grief

let it all flow into my eternal waters
where it will be returned as love

stay as long as you need
until you are done letting go
and then stay some more

drink in my light
drink in my love

rest your heavy head
find solace in my womb

surrender and sleep

and when you are ready

only when you feel strong
when you feel whole

stand up and dance on my shores

I am the calm and peaceful lake
the place inside you
where you are unconditionally loved
where you can never do wrong

the infinite space
where you
and your soul
are one

I Hoped to Arrive a Dazzling Queen

I hoped to come to you
glowing, iridescent, and pure
hair braided with ribbons of gold
skin glistening with morning dew

I hoped to knock on your castle door
draped in my finest garments
crowned with fresh flowers
smelling of lavender perfumes

I hoped to bow at your feet
offering the cleanest version of me
bedecked in sparkling jewels

I hoped to arrive a dazzling queen

but it's been such a journey
getting to you

I am here
but with my hair wild, wiry, and messy
with my muddy feet caked in earth

I am here

but with tear-stained and tired
circles under my eyes
snot dripping from my nose

I am here
having crawled most of the way
smudged in dirt and grime
in tattered rags
knees scraped and covered in blood

I am here
I dragged myself to you
using all my courage and strength
a million obstacles
held me down
pulled me back
but I flung each one away
with my inner flame
with my love of you

nothing stopped me from finding you
nothing could have stopped me
from seeing you every step of the way

with my sword of truth
I slashed away all doubt
I fought through every darkness

through thickly thorned forests of despair
ignoring all the lies tearing at my flesh

I never stopped reaching you

I am here
a battle-worn mess
but not broken
still whole
trusting you know my heart
trusting you see my soul

I am here
trusting you see
the space inside me
I have kept free
to receive
to be filled

I am here
having surrendered
having offered all my darkness
all my light

I am here
an empty chalice
for unconditional love

perhaps
I am arriving
a dazzling queen after all

I'm Not Pretending Anymore

I'm not pretending anymore
to be a victim of my love

I'm not pretending anymore
not to be me

I've cried as if I'm sad
I've cried as if I'm lost

but now I know that's just
my crazy open heart

I'm not pretending anymore
that I don't know who I am

that power within me
(that comes from beyond me)
doesn't want to be held back

I'm ready to let it out!
and break you wide apart

and if you let my light in
this life will be a dream

set aflame
with the sacred feminine

I am Divine Mother
I am Kali Ma
I am Shakti
I am Cosmic Energy

now let me reign!

and make no mistake
I love no matter what

by the fire of the spirit
in the palace of the heavens
I will wait for you to come

and once you're in my arms
you will rest with me forever
protected by undying love

How Can You Expect Me to Act Sane?

how can you expect me to act sane?

I tell you

what I have seen in the light
dancing on the surface of the ocean
what I have seen in the stars
on a moonless night
what I have seen nestled
among the petals of a rose
is enough to make me
mad with ecstasy

what I have heard in the silence of dawn
in the pauses between the holy man's chants
in the symphony of birds
calling me to the day
in the gentle rustle of leaves
is plenty to make me
howl like a lunatic

what I have felt in the wind's cool caress of
my cheek
when I run my fingers through a kitten's fur

in the warm sand beneath my feet
in the luxury of a velvet leaf
is enough to make me
babble endlessly with bliss

what I have tasted as I bit into a pear
as I sipped on a cup of decadent cacao
as I licked sweet honey off my lips
as I indulged in a persimmon or a fig
is all I need to make me
sing as if deranged

what I have smelled in a bundle of sage
in a pine forest on a crisp sunny day
in the earth after it rains
in a lavender bouquet
is enough to make me
never be normal again

and I tell you

what I have seen
in your eyes as you look into mine
what I have heard in your voice
when you speak my name
what I have felt in your palms
against my skin

what I have tasted on your lips
when we kiss
what I have smelled in your skin
when we embrace
is more than enough to make me
lose my mind
with knowing God

so how, oh how,
can you expect me to act sane?

A Man Who Will Pleasure in Poetry

I want a man who will pleasure in poetry
with me

he will understand the poetry of dead men
and the poetry of mountains and trees

he will stay up all night poring over sacred
texts with me, those poems written by Hafiz,
Kabir, and Rumi and those written by God
onto the length of my body

he will never bore of Whitman or
Wordsworth and will know by heart the poem
of a rose and never tire of memorizing the
poetry of me

he will understand that to dance
is to shout odes to the heavens

and that silence is a haiku
worshipping creation

he will hear the sonnets sung by rivers and
streams and the ballads carried by the winds

he will hush the whole world to honor the
limericks of birds

he will whisper Neruda's words into my ears
and press Shakespeare onto my lips

he will lean in to listen to the metaphors my
soul whispers

and open his heart to let me read the secrets
he's scribbled there

he will know that to make love is to write
epics, is to rival Homer, Milton, Cervantes!

and he will see the universe in a word and the
cosmos in a leaf

he will know that when we express the ecstasy
of our love, angels in heaven pull up a seat to
listen raptly to us just *be*

he will know that as we walk down the street

(or when we merely *breathe*)

we leave a trail of glorious verse in our wake

I want a man who will pleasure in poetry
with me

The Top of the Mountain

hand over hand
foot over foot
I climb
to the top of the mountain
and to my astonishment
there at the top
calm and silent
you sit
smiling
waiting for me
and I realize
what in my heart
I have known all along:
there has always, ever,
and only
been
one of us here

Worship

Mother Earth, I worship you
I fall on my knees in humble servitude
I throw your dirt around me in ecstasy!

I bathe myself in sage
in lavender
in roses
I wrap myself in leaves and wind
I braid your butterflies and stars
into my hair

I open my heart
I expose my bare breast
and let all of you in!

shatter me with your love!
expand me with your life force!

I bow at your feet
I worship all your creation
I see myself in *all*
and I worship *me*

and I kiss every inch

of the body in front me
I press his heart to mine
for he is me
I remember
he is the whole universe
manifest in one body
for me to love relentlessly

I worship you!
I worship me!
and by my love
I make
all sacred
around me

Walking in the Beauty Way

we have found our voices
but what does that mean?

we don't need to say everything

there are lessons from the past
about the power of silence
the power of listening

let's keep our hearts open

let's remember what we wanted all along

to create beauty with our songs
to delight in our bodies' freedom
to celebrate by dancing
to teach with our kindness

with our love

to worship and make sacred
all we touch

to leave a trail

of highest truth
in our wake

as we tread lightly
on this holy Earth

Gratitude

thank you, Beloved,
for setting me free
to know what's
not for me

thank you, my love,
for helping me
let go of the story
while keeping
all the love
flowing through me

thank you, Beloved,
for the pain
the sting
that taught me
what was no longer
working for me

thank you, my love,
for releasing me
from the old ways
of thinking
and for finally

allowing me to breathe

you didn't even know
you were doing it
but you reminded me:
I'm infinitely capable
of creating
and spreading beauty

thank you, Beloved!
through you
I was able
to set
myself
free!

Like a Butterfly

do you remember that time
we created our own realm?
you were king
and I was queen
and we made a heaven
where we reigned

we summitted mountains
and ran down them
laughing in the rain

remember when we sat around the fire
created from the love we gave so freely?
you played your drum
to the beat of our hearts
and I sang with a voice
I didn't know I had
until I set it free
knowing with you
I could be all of me

remember when you made up that story
about the boy and the tree?
to calm my heart and help me sleep?

remember the poetry we read?
the feasts of love we indulged in?

all the while it rained outside
a wall of water protecting what we built

remember telling me
that someday you'd travel
just you and your guitar?
that someday you'd have a garden
filled with exotic flowers?
and me saying all I want
is to worship every sacred moment?
and you answering,
"I think you're almost there"?

remember how I drank you in
and filled my heart
knowing every little thing about you
was a message for me?

we were children at play
teaching each other true love
learning what it means to be divine
in the presence of the Divine

expecting nothing

giving everything

was it just a fleeting moment?
like a butterfly landing on a leaf?
a beautiful lesson lasting a second
then flying to the next thing?

our realm does live on in me
I go there sometimes
to remember
what that butterfly taught me
hoping that in that dream
we will again meet

I know we cannot look back
that we must trust in our magic
keep creating heaven
on our separate paths
keep flowing
down the glorious river of life
seeing God in all things

but I cannot lie
I cannot say that I don't hope
that around this river bend
or the next one
I will see you again

standing there in your special way
so centered in yourself
strong and straight
waiting for me

like the diagram you drew
two lines intersecting
here ... and there

is it wrong for me
to believe in the moment
to envision the point

when again our paths will meet?

Look at Your Feet

what are you striving for?

let go of all goals
let go of all ambitions
let go of what you think
you have to become

you are already here
you are already what you seek

look at your feet

you have already arrived
just breathe
and remember
the life that you are

it is in you
it is all around you

open your heart
open your cells
let it all be
let it flow through

the channels of your being
feel the humble immensity
of who you are
and everything
you are a part of

there are no boundaries
and yet
you are self-contained
in your beautiful body

step by step
always arriving
with every breath saying:

I am here
I am here
I am here

there is only *now*
there is only *love*
there is only *presence*

it is everything

take it all in

you know
you know
you know

now be *it*

the answer is in you
the answer is *you*

amen
hallelujah
sat nam

om

shanti shanti shanti

and deepest profoundest gratitude

now go on
and in the beauty way

be free

lokah somastah sukhino bhavantu

what else is there to say?

This Thisness

there are no words for
this thisness

this space between
inhale and exhale

this answer to all things
in the void

this everything
in the nothing

this nothing
in the everything

this being
this ineffable something
which I honor above all things

this thisness

expanding me infinitely
into a gratitude
no words can contain

An Unraveling

an unraveling is taking place
deep inside me
extending to the *cosmos*

a beautiful dismantling
of all that I thought was me
of all that I thought wasn't me

a wondrous disintegration of old ways
held onto for far too long
holding me/you/us back for lifetimes

a massive spring cleaning
going into the deepest corners
of the hidden closets of my being

sweeping out all
the long-forgotten patterns
a making way, a making space

creating emptiness
a void for the birth of new creation
an "everything must go" clearance sale

to be *free*!

an unraveling is taking place
and I am absolutely getting out of its way

I Can No Longer Write Poems

I can no longer write poems
about your splendor

I lie in this darkness
enveloped in your love

but the word "love"?
meaningless!

I lie in this darkness
enveloped in you

you?

no

it's the feeling of
knowing—
            knowing!

there is nothing *but* you
knowing—
            knowing!

you are always with me

even that sounds absurd

"with me"?

we have dissolved
into each other

I can no longer pick apart
the parts that are you
the parts that are me

nor do I want to waste any energy
on that deciphering

so let me just lie here
bathing in our beauty
bathing in our existence/non-existence

for I no longer know anything
but this being
            nothing
                        and everything
in you

words have disintegrated

a pile of ash

pointing at nothing

and so

I can no longer write poems

so what is this?
I'm not sure

but then again

I know it's me

I know it's you

I know this feeling

my compass

when words
lose all meaning

and though you do not know you love me
and may never realize it in this lifetime

I am glad!
that my eyes were opened
to the magnificence of you

I have come to know
the divinity of every creature

but there are those special people
that because of their special way
of being in this world
appeal to my soul

in just the right way

and they open my heart
to the abundance of existence
the love of creation

and though they may never fall
off the same cliff
they have pushed me off of

I am grateful they helped me
excavate the depths of me
discover more of what's inside me

and you, my darling,
are just such a being

because of you I swim

yes, I swim
(and almost melt!)
in the warm goo
the love
this blissful *isness*
that is the core of me

and suddenly poems pour
in and out of me

and I am dancing

and do I care what got me here?

who said unrequited love
must be oh so painful?

I joy in it

like a fish
thrown back
into the ocean

Witness Me

I have spent
so much time

longing

to be seen

my soul crying:

witness me!
see how resplendent I am!
see how amazing this body is!
the way it moves!
the way all the pieces fit together!
every hair just so!
see how these fingers gesture!
see these hips dance!
see how this mouth forms words!
how this heart beats!
what about these crazy toes!
these wild eyes shining!
these songs that are sung!

see all the ways

that this being
does the things she does!
is she not magnificent?!
see me!

but now
I sit silent,
and still
because I know

all creation witnesses me

God witnesses me

I witness me!

and the more
I witness me

the more
I witness you.

The Purest Honey

this is about you and me, love
yes! you and me!
us two
us one now

I don't know
if you see it
but try
to feel it!

we have become
the purest honey

you and me, love

well
that's not exactly true
is it?

no becoming was needed

this sweetness has always been
an eternal flow

a divine liquid gold

pouring into you
out of me

pouring into me
out of you

yes! you and me, love!

never ceasing to be
the sweetest alchemy

Here I Am

and so all there is left
is to sink ever more deeply
into the moment

don't rush to leave this now
don't escape into the future
don't long for the past

the only thing to do
(because you've tried
everything else and—
face it—none of it helped)
is sink

       even

            more

                  deeply

into the moment

into this now
and everything it contains
let it swallow you whole
until you are no more

until all that's left

is this everything
this simultaneous
you and not you

yes
just let it
swallow you whole

breathe into this moment
until all you are is

om

Harvest Time

come home, my love!
you have traveled long enough
it's time now
for the harvest of this love
I have grown
from the soils of my soul
nourished with the radiance of my heart
and watered
with the tears of my joy
      at seeing you in all things!

I am ready now
to receive you in my arms
these branches are laden with fruit
bursting with sweet sticky juices
come home, my love!
and let me flow over you
come home, my love!
      I am ripe for the picking

Glorious Leaves

everyone loves autumn trees
their golden brown and rusty leaves
falling away
crackling in the wind
and under our feet

we sigh,
"how beautiful nature planned it all to be"

I hope that when you gaze upon me
in the autumn of my years
you see me as a tree
silver grays and crow's feet
my glorious leaves

I hope you sigh,
"how beautiful nature planned it all to be"

seasons changing perfectly

Back to School

I retreat within—

into the jungle
of my soul

I go
and sit there
in silence
until even
my breath
disappears

in this precious
moment
ineffable
truth
permeates
my being

(you've felt it too,
I'm sure)

I return
to the world

master
of myself
knowing
what I need
to know:

I am
unstoppable
love

but soon, too soon
the thickness
of experience
slowly
veils my eyes

soon, too soon
I'm lost
in the world again
face planted
in egoic illusions

oh well,
I smile

back to school
I go

who really
wants to be done
learning anyway?

Desert Festival

last night
here
in the spacious heart of the desert
I hosted a festival,
a gathering to celebrate
the richness of this life

you might say:
"but I drove by
and it was just you sitting
beneath the sky"

ah, you see—
the gathering was inside of me
and all my best friends came:
the stars, the moon,
sages from far and wide
some from a long ago time

Mother Earth showed up, too
queen of the feast
she sat on her throne
in my heart
smiling

presiding over the night

the dancing was wild

the singing
glorious

the conversation
absurd

the laughter
deep and full

drunk on nothing
but sweet company,
we reveled for hours

colors swirling
all of us twirling
until ecstasy
reached its natural height

dawn came
my guests
went their way
(or maybe never left)

but trust me

there sure was
a festival
here last night

At the Ball

in my dreams
last night
I was Cinderella
dancing at the ball

everything
glimmered and twinkled
I lived in a world
where everyone
sparkled like a diamond
and jewels fell
from the sky

I could have stayed forever
in that place
where my heart
was a million times its size

but I woke up today
a pumpkin again

I sighed and thought:
"of course, it can't be that way"

until I looked
in your eyes
and saw that
we always carry
magic inside

Apple Picking

I went apple picking
in the orchard of my mind

there I picked an apple
just like *you*
golden and glowing
it had everything inside

a gift for you
I carry in my heart

waiting
for the moment
when like Eve
I tempt you
to take a bite

Hauntings

sometimes I'm not sure
I can afford to love again

I have buried so many men
in the cemetery of my desires

and damn it!
they all keep rising from the dead

if it's not one, it's the other
haunting my heart

in the night
I hear their soft howling

they whisper in my ears
and rattle through my bones

throughout the day
they startle me

sudden ghastly apparitions
amidst my thoughts and chores

memories send shivers
chilling me to my core

it's not their fault, really
that they are my ghosts
it's me who can't let go
of those feelings so old

all those kisses
all those caresses
all those moments
that left me naked
in body and soul

yet I know
I am still expanding

so I can sit with these hauntings
so I can let them live inside me

I am allowing them to teach me
that love is also in the letting go

that though a relationship ends
the connection never ceases

and we can always take in more

Fall Wedding

On these autumnal days
I go skipping down the street
in love with everything
and I daydream—

Why not have a fall wedding?
I'm ready to celebrate
a sacred union within

Let's wed my yin to my yang
my sun to my moon
my high to my low
my shadow to my goodness

We'll have it in the forest
witnessed by my friends, the trees,
decorated by the falling leaves

We'll feast on pumpkin pie,
butternut squash,
sweet pears, crisp apples—
drink flowing golden cider, too

We'll have cinnamon kisses

and hot cocoa embraces

We'll dance all night
beneath the hunter's moon
and sing true love songs
while a banjo twangs out tunes

And as the sun comes up
we'll huddle together
creature and human alike
around a glowing fire
generated by our hearts

Why not have a fall wedding?
I'll be the bride
and I'll be the groom

My Mother

my Mother
she calls to me

a good daughter
I cannot ignore her
for too long

the mountain pulls me
a magnet to my heart

to the trail I must go
to pay my respects

to my Mother
who gives to me
boundlessly

for her
I climb to the summit

with her
I watch the sunset

to her

I howl at the moon

I grow silent and still
I bend my ear to the ground

deeply I listen to her wisdom
hidden in the pulse of life

I recognize the wind
as her endless loving caress

I breathe in
I breathe out

this is how I pray in her temple
this is how I thank her

A Strange Kind of Pilgrim

I am a strange kind of pilgrim

traveling far
eternally
in the blink of an eye

I am a strange kind of pilgrim

so often lost
so often forgetting
I'm on a path at all

I am a strange kind of pilgrim

my journey
just remembering
I already am
where I want to go

I am a strange kind of pilgrim

my destination
fidelity
to love

The Lilies in the Field

Benjamin Franklin wisely said:
"by failing to prepare,
we are preparing to fail"

dear old Ben,
I don't disagree with you,
but I am trying
something new these days

I've spent so much
life and energy
preparing to not fail,
believing I was
in control of things

and if you look at
the evidence, perhaps
all that effort paid off

I'm still here after all
and doing quite well

but maybe,
everything would

have turned out
quite all right
no matter what?

maybe, if I'd let go of the reins just a bit,
maybe, if I'd trusted in fate just a bit,
maybe, if I'd trusted in God a lot,
everything would have
still been ok
but with a little more
fun along the way

so I'm trying to be
a little more like
those lilies in the field
that never worry
about anything
they just radiate beautifully
and let God take care of everything

don't worry, Ben,
it's just an experiment
I'll admit it sounds scary

but I think it's worth a try

Coquí Frogs

there's a place
on the Big Island
where thousands
of tiny coquí frogs'
mating calls
can be heard all night

there,
you lie
beneath the sequined sky
you and the universe
and the relentless noise
of the littlest frogs

it's beautiful
and it's intense

and although
at times
you crave silence,
you realize
that though
you could hush them
if you wished,

you wouldn't dare
disturb the cosmic balance
that a wiser you put in place,
you would never ask
the flow of life
to take a pause,
no matter what
your personal wants are

so
you lie back
spread your arms out wide
and call to the love
you are ready to embrace:

come, all you little annoying
yet exquisite coquí frogs!

come, all you manifestations
of God's grace!

kiss my body
all over the place!

to all of it!

I say yes!

Am I Love?

I stood in the light
but now
I stand beneath a gloomy sky
and lift my eyes up to cry:

am I love?!

you have told me I am

and even in this dark hour
something deep inside me
pounds out a primal reminder:

yes

yes

yes

yes

you are

I beat my chest to the rhythm

to get past the old fear
that has crept in unnoticed
amidst my busy day

once again
I allowed
the world to cloud
my view of the truth

once again
I became preoccupied
with the whispers and shouts
of my lesser self
whose voice makes me doubt
who I am

love?

I'm not sure that is what I am
but I know where to seek the reminder:

deep deep inside of me
beyond the valleys of darkness
where I grope in blindness
I will find
that secret treasure
always pulsating

never ceasing
beating out that ancient chant:

I am love

I am life

I am truth

I am

as surely as I breathe
this is all that I can be

and a voice
in that place
within me
whispers:

it's ok
that you call on me

your Mother
your Queen
your Self

to remind you

again and again

yes

my darling
precious
angel

you are love

Brainwashing

does brainwashing have to be
a bad thing?

because I often feel
desperately in need
of a good
thorough
washing
a downright
scrubbing
of my brain

I even say to my teacher
my heart
to the Self I know
is watching over me:

please, please, brainwash me!

wash away the lies I tell me

wash away the false stories
repeating endlessly
in the hallways of my mind

wash it all away!

give me a *deep* cleaning
so I can start anew
and believe the things
my heart knows are true

oh, my heart!

wash away the residue
of my old ways
I trust in you

I surrender
to your kind
of brainwashing
through and through

yes, I believe
brainwashing
can be good

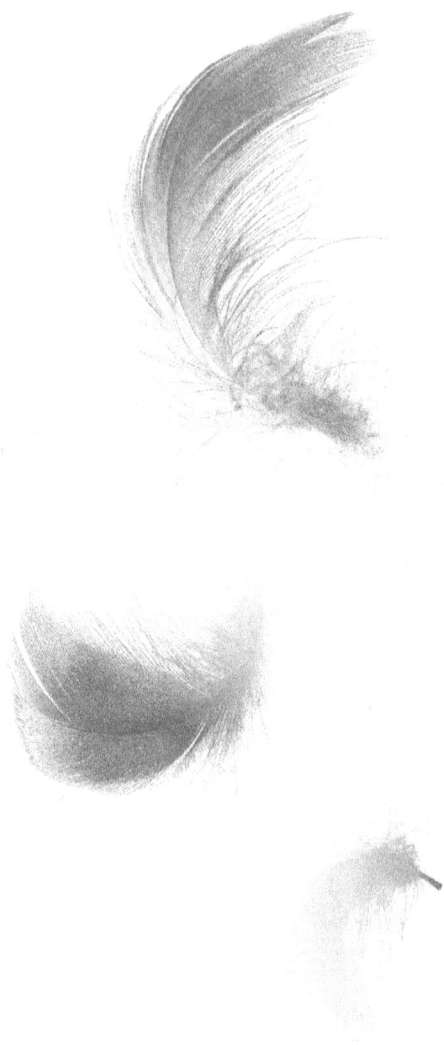

I'm No Saint

I'm no saint
for sure

it is an unholy
unclean
goddamn messy
temple
that I occupy

and yet

every breath
I draw
is sacred

and the love
I give
is pure
and true

Small Talk and Opinions

dearest

I beg you
see through my charade
this silly act of mine
expose me
as the lover I am
strip me naked
so I stand
just a hollow form,
my purpose only one:
reverberating forever
this simple love

my deepest desire
is that when you hear me speak
you recognize every word
that slips passed my lips
as a cleverly disguised
"I love you"

And the spaces between the words
as silently whispered
"thank yous"

the small talk?
the passionate opinions?
they are but thin veils
barely hiding
this endless echo,
this infinite symphony
of "thank you, I love you"
that your gorgeous existence
inspires my soul to sing

I Am a Pioneer

it's impossible
for you to know
how much
I love you
because every day
I am discovering
new spaces inside me
filled with love of you

I am a pioneer
trekking
through the wilderness
of my soul
and every day
I stand on the threshold
of a new frontier
looking out onto new horizons

and I will never cease exploring
this lawless void
this boundless unknown
this uncharted land

because whenever I wonder:

when will I reach
the limits of this love?

something out there
from the eternal vastness answers:
never
never
there is *always* more love

Portal to Love

when we met
I knew
you were one
of my angels

I knew
because your eyes
your words
your existence
opened new places
inside me
and flooded them
with love

and still
even
when we are apart
just the thought of you
serves as
a portal to love

I can just step through
and I am bathed
in truth

when I remember you
I remember me

simply put,
I am grateful
for the gift
that is you

Om

now that I know love
the word itself has become so small
and yet

how else can I describe
this feeling
this experience
this state
this something
permeating everything?

what sound
coming from these human lips
could possibly encapsulate
the immensity
of this truth of all things?

awwww?
mmmmm?
oooooh?

oh!

om

Sorry Not Sorry

here is my confession:

I have been dishonest with you

I have a secret agenda

I am using you

you should know
nothing I do is innocent
or pure

I am exploiting you
(and all of creation)
to gain access to my True Love
my Beloved who waits for me
in every atom
in every millisecond
with open arms
calling my name
incessantly

every move I make
is a calculated

expanding
of my heart
into love

a leaning in to know you
to better know me
to better know love

a burning away
of all the things
between me and the shore
where my Beloved
sits patiently

I am using you

it's not personal

I am just an opportunist

every word
every action
every thing
everywhere
offers
an opportunity
to open more

to get to that other shore

even this
is a part of that undertaking

maybe
by standing this naked
I will fall
(finally!)
into that ocean
of divine love—
never to emerge separate again

I am using you

there you are
standing before me
in all your majesty
and I cannot help but see
you are my opportunity

you are not in my way
you are the way

and I am ruthless
in my quest

so I am sorry not sorry

I ask your forgiveness
though I cannot change

but I can offer you this in return:

please for God's sake
feel free
to use me
in the same way

Under the Trees

I want to be as a tree

that is evolution

grounded in the earth
reaching for the Divine
connected above and below

roots crawling
towards everything
entangled in everything
branches expanding
holding hands
never knowing
where one ends
and another begins

sheltering
providing
for all who seek
solace
refuge
home

I am home under the trees
leaning my weary body
against their solidity

so if I can't be a tree
I will live in their branches
climb up into their arms
and be enveloped with leaves

walk this world looking up
at their green canopy

all that love
watching over me

Falling (Deeply) in Love

I gathered the courage
of a thousand tigers

took a breath

and stepped into the well

arms stretched above me
legs dangling below me

I fell

into the void

allowing
allowing

I fell endlessly

deeper and deeper
I went

I watched
the pain and the glory

swirling all around me
my heart grew
to contain
the wondrous madness

deeper and deeper
I went

a smile spread across my lips
a giggle rose from my soul

I sighed with pleasure

as I realized to my joy
the well was bottomless
an eternal void

I would be
falling
falling

falling in love

forever

I Say Yes!

yes!
I say yes!

yes!
to the pain

yes!
to the suffering

yes!
to the struggle

yes!
to the never-ending
expansion
of me

yes!
let's do this!
let's see!
how much life we can take
how much love we can be

yes!

to everything!
the horror
the beauty
the Infinite Sea
that is all of me

yes!
I spread my arms
I stretch myself
to embrace
the majesty
the energy
the lifeforce
within me
all around me

yes!
take me!
destroy me!
love me!
in all the ways

yes!
I am here
for it all

yes! yes! yes!

please come with me!
there is room for us all

It's True, My Love

it's true, my love, that someday I'll be gone
it's true that someday you will be gone, too
and this beautiful blossoming flower
before us?
she, too, will have withered and moved on

but
in the now
I am here
in the now
you are here
and in the now
this precious flower
in all its many-petalled splendor
is here as well

so let us delight in this richness

allow me to hold your hand, my love
and together
let's fall deeply
into the infinite expanse
of this single miraculous moment

let's let this wondrous flower
bring us to our knees
let's plummet fearlessly
into awe and celebration
until there's nothing left to feel

don't let go of me
and I won't let go of you

let's breathe together
let's let life fill all the spaces
around us and within us
let's not stop
until we know
every precious petal of existence

because

now

now

now

we are here

Teach Me, Sisters

teach me, sisters
how to live firmly in this body
worship every cell
how to carry myself with humble grace
how to allow
all my imperfections and flaws
and embrace them
with strength and confidence

teach me, sisters
how to connect
with my womb
how to create
beauty in all I do
how to wield
the power of my voice
and be impeccable
with all my words

teach me, sisters
how to walk
with Mother Earth
how to breathe
in harmony with her

how to make every inhale a prayer
and every exhale a sigh of gratitude

teach me, sisters
how to let everything go
and flow like water
how to dance
like a madwoman around the fire
how to let my roots ground me
in the earth
and to expand like air
and be everywhere

teach me, sisters
how to tenderly hold another's pain
how to love even when it hurts like hell
how to take care of those around me
and not spread my energy too thin

teach me, sisters
how to transmute and tame my rage
how to be both gentle and fierce
how to balance my yin and my yang
and to maintain a sacred union within

teach me, sisters
how to honor who I am and bravely shine

how to sit and revel in our collective light
how to truly be alive and free
and yet maintain the balance of reciprocity

teach me, sisters
how to love both you and me better
how to accept all the parts of everything
how to keep love alive in every moment
and how to stand up for my sisters and my
brothers

please teach me, sisters!
how to listen
to the wisdom of the universe
how to never stop opening my heart
how to remember
that the learning never ends
and there always will be
new lessons to unlock

I Am Magnificent

I am here
to claim
my magnificence

I have climbed this steep mountain of doubt
and now I stand upright on its peak,
shoulders back, chin strong,
staring down my fear

my mane blowing in the wind,
the sun beaming on my skin,
I spread my arms
like eagle's wings

I roar with the voice of the lioness in me:
I am magnificent!

I proclaim it for myself and for all to hear

I own it in every cell of my body

I say it again
with the strength of all creation backing me
and lifeforce filling my entire being:

I AM MAGNIFICENT!

I am here to claim it
so that *you*, my love,
can claim
your magnificence, too

In This Traveling Temple

I have discovered
a temple
that rivals
the one Solomon built

this temple
is not visible
to the naked eye

but to those
who use their hearts to see
it is more apparent
than anything
on this plane of reality

this temple
can never
be torn down

because
its walls are fluid
always moving,
the divinest music,
the songs of those

who have made solemn vows
to be warriors
of truth
and love
every note
extending
endlessly
expanding this temple
made of harmony

there is no roof
on this temple of mine
so that we can look up
and remember who we are

every morning
there are prayer services
led by birds and angels
and together we worship
the rising sun

every night
we gather in praise
with all of creation
howling our thanks
for the glorious gifts
of another day done

but also
in this temple
every moment
is an open-eyed meditation

honoring this *now*
this piece of earth
where my feet stand

and all day long
in this temple
a fire is kept alive
by those who have
sworn to never let
the flames of Spirit die

and the doors of this temple,
the doors of my heart,
are always wide open
welcoming all

to dance with me!
like wild children of the Divine

or to kneel with me
bowing our heads
in silent

reverent
immeasurable
gratitude
to all Creation
to all that we are

this dancing
this kneeling
is always going on

in this traveling temple
that goes wherever
I am

You Make It Easy

before I get into it
before I begin
I need to make something clear

just this once
I don't want to leave
any room for interpretation
I don't want there to be
any misunderstanding

and I don't want you
wiggling away
from the fact
that this poem
is about you

this is me
reaching out
grabbing you by the shirt
looking you in the eye
and telling you:

this is
most

definitely
about you

the you
that is reading this
the you
that by some cosmic chance
found these words

incredible
magical
you

don't worry about the parts
that make you doubt
that make you think
"that doesn't sound like me"
or seem to be describing
someone else

this is
most certainly
about *you*

so let's begin:

last night

sitting in darkness
I contemplated you

I thought about each
of the millions of cells
that make up you

I imagined the eons of events
that amounted to the pattern
of atoms that is you

I marveled
at the ongoing evolution
that is you

precisely
specifically
you

I had the best time
getting lost
in all your details

the dark pools of your eyes
the curve of your smile
the slope of your extraordinary nose
the slenderness of your fingers

that little-bit-larger bone on your wrist
the way your hair sometimes
stands out in every direction

every perfectly placed
line of your body
every perfectly vibrating
part of your soul

the way you walk?
every step an intention

and your laugh?
WOW—
it expands me
times a million

and your heart?
a lighthouse inside you
always aflame
no matter your mood

the way you regret mistakes
the pain you express

the so-unique train of your thoughts
how you pause before you talk

and say every word
like you're giving birth
to something precious and new

but
the truth is

I wanna erase
everything
I just said about you

I wanna just lie back in the grass
and forget words
because there is no way
I can explain
the exquisiteness that is you

it would take volumes
I would have to start at the top of your head
and work my way down to your toes
millimeter by millimeter
to not miss anything
and I would have to stop
in between every millimeter
to admire all that is unseen

it would take lifetimes

to itemize the essence of you

and I know
I still would never get it right

I've already tried too hard
this has gone on for far too long

because it's not your individual parts
or even the combination
of your virtues and flaws
it's not anything I could list on paper

you are a masterpiece
of creation

and when I just relax
lie back in the grass
to conjure you?
the entirety of the constantly
changing energy that is you?

I am sublime

I am alive

I fall into vastness

I fall into the energy
that binds everything

I fall in love

I dwell in love

in a way I never knew
never understood
until I saw you
until I realized
I would
never
never
change anything
about you

that I would be happy
just sitting in darkness
eternally contemplating
you
forever enjoying
you

and don't worry
you don't owe me
anything

because loving
admiring
glorying
in all of you
all of me
all of everything
is what I most like to do

thank you!

you make it easy

so easy

to be in love

with you

with me

with everything

and isn't it interesting?
that maybe
this poem

isn't about you?

it seems
it might be about me

but I'm you after all

you make that easy to see

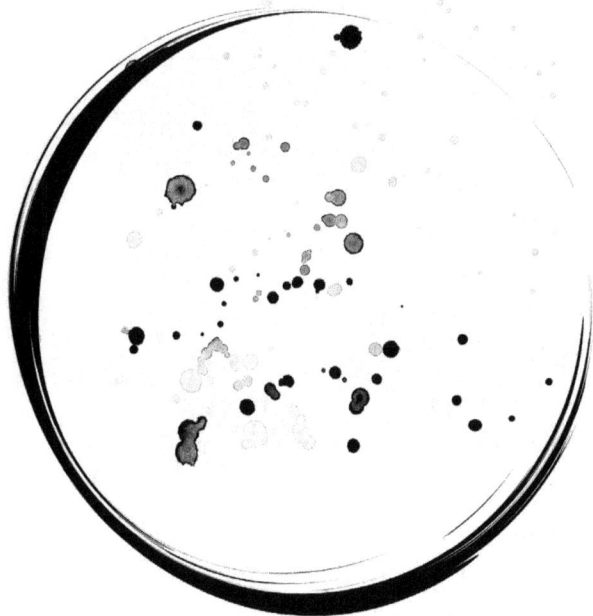

That Slippery Fish Called Truth

yesterday I held her
that slippery fish called Truth
I held her for just a little bit longer
but long enough to memorize
her exact shape with my hands
long enough to commit the texture
of her shimmering scales
to the memory of my heart
long enough to feel
how perfectly she sits
in the empty space inside me
(that place I keep empty for her)

I had only a sliver of a window
the tiniest portal
to stay with her
to not frighten her
to expand that sliver into infinity

presence

presence

presence

listen

listen

listen

to the wisdom

beyond time

beyond space

that knowledge that is so fleeting
that knowledge that can't be contained

the trick?

to hold her
but not squeeze her
to be with her
but allow her
to be anything

to *feel*
to learn
but not try to capture
with the mind

like a steel trap

to not build her a prison of words

to know
but not think I've completely understood
she who is the ultimate mystery

to see her
to *feel* her
in all her glory
but to never limit her

to just

open

open

open

continuously open

so I must be careful
this slippery fish is so sensitive
to the slightest muscle twitch
hinting at contraction

hinting at capture

she'll be gone in an instant

but now
I have memorized her curves
looked into her eyes
(those infinite pools)
and known what it is
to be dazzled by her love

my body remembers
what it means to merge
with the essence that is her

and though I
cannot tell you any details
cannot tell you how to meet her
cannot draw you a portrait or a map
to where she waits for you

I do know what is *not* her
I am not fooled by poor imitations
and my body
my heart
my soul
has memorized its way back to her

(even if I can only visit for a second)

and maybe
just maybe

if we sit here together
so patient
so still
so surrendered
with no expectations
that she'll return

maybe
just maybe

we can have that moment
where something opens
and suddenly see
that she,

that slippery fish,
with her ever-shifting
always subtly swishing
iridescent being

has always been here
swimming

in that vast ocean
within

Making Love

for lifetimes
I have desired you
the experience of your love
craved to be filled by you
from pinky toe to crown

and only today
(while basking in the morning sun)
did it really dawn on me
did it really hit me over the head

finally

finally

I understood

to know the vastness of your love
I must drop the limits of who I am
rid myself of all identities
leave no boundaries between us

forget my own name!

empty myself completely
only then
will I be open to infinite ecstasy

only then
will we be making love
you and me
one endless merging sea

Rumi and Me

there's nowhere left to turn
but the poems of Rumi

him and me
we have an understanding

he gets me
he knows
how it is to be
in love
all the time
with all of everything
always on the edge
of ecstasy

his poems rise
from the pages
to embrace me
I am held close
and I hear
the heartbeat
behind his words
whispering:

yes
yes
yes

what you're feeling
is absolutely true

Talking to You about the Weather

here I am again
talking to you about the weather

despite the truth
that all I really want
is to say:
I love you

and explain just
how spectacular
you are

I guess
I'm not sure
you're ready for that
I'm not sure
you'd understand me
clearly
if I really spoke my heart
it might be too easy
for you to think
I want to put you away
in a gilded cage
and keep you for mine

(like Pablo Neruda wanted
to do with his socks*)
you might not realize I'm in love all the time
and though you *are*
a magnificent and unique manifestation
of love on my path
a convergence of energy attracting my heart,
you're also not special

that's what we all are

and yet
inside me
I am down on my knees
thanking the universe
that it chose
incredible you
to teach me

love

and I want to grab you by the shoulders
and shake you hard
I want to hold your gaze
past all the awkward moments

---

* "Ode to My Socks" by Pablo Neruda

and just shout:

"WOW! here we are! you and me!
holy shit! how lucky am I?"

but again
I don't know
if you're ready for that
(I'm not
underestimating you—
it just might be
too much right now)

plus maybe

silence
is the best way
to communicate
these thoughts

for now
I'll hang back
and trust
that you
already know,
in your soul
that in me

is an infinite spring
gushing
with love
for all you are

so
here I am
talking to you about the weather

winking at you
with everything I've got

Love Is a Collapsing

I once thought
love was *some thing*
something to receive
something to give
something to earn
something to deserve

I thought
it was *some thing*
that looked a certain way
that only existed
under certain
circumstances

I thought
love was *some thing*
between two people
something to wait for

I thought
love was *some thing*
that made you mine
that said you had to do this or that
because you said, "I love you"

over time
I realized
love was *some thing*
inside me
something I could
create
generate
something I could choose
something I could give myself
over and over again
no matter what

I realized
there was no waiting
for love to come
to find me

and that felt
pretty good
this self-love

I thought I knew
what it was to be in love
with me
with everything
I was pretty proud
thought I had it figured out

but then
some force
from heaven
knocked me on my knees
showed me how small
I was thinking

love is not *some thing*

it is not something
to give or choose

love is seeing
there is nothing
to be taken
or given

no plusses
no minuses

love is absolute

love is freedom
love is presence
love is what is

all there is

love is every cell in the body
vibrating "yes" to the world

love is opening your arms
as wide as the sky

love is the perfection
of all creation

love is the infinite majesty
embracing all reality

love is God
love is now
love is energy

God is love
now is love
energy is love

love *is*

is love

love is the absurdity
of me trying to communicate

love is all words

disintegrating

love is a chiseling away
of all that is not me

love is a collapsing

of giving
and receiving
into one
eternal
reciprocity

an opening up
to let energy
flow freely

infinite availability

trusting deeply

moving
moving

believing

that there really is
only
just
one
thing

actually
nothing

no thing
that is everything

a collapsing

into singularity

and if you're
understanding
any of this

thank God!
for your
precious heart

because I
no longer know
what to say

love is a collapsing

of mind into soul

so please
sit here
with me
in this space
beyond words

help me
always
remember

love is
just
holding
hands
with the world

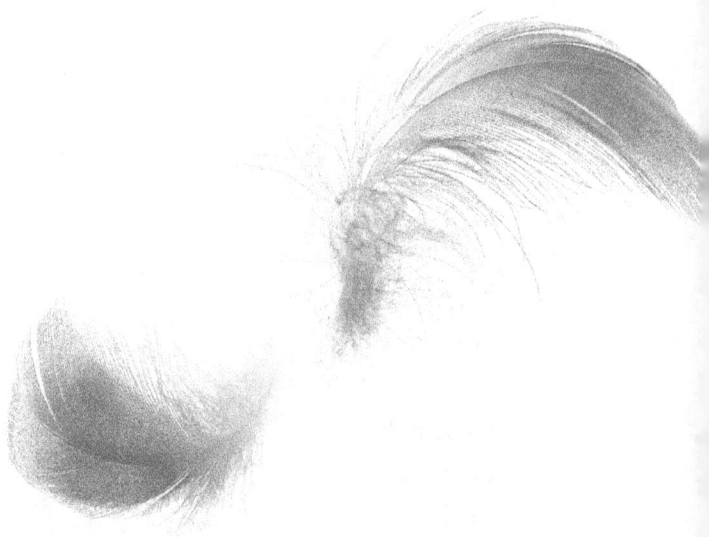

Saying the Same Thing

by now
you've probably seen
right through me and my "art"

realized that
I have not so secretly
been saying the same thing
all along:

I love you
thank you
we're one

that's all

but if you're like me
you need to be
hit over the head
more than once

if you're like me
it takes a while
for things to sink in
to listen with all your heart

if you're like me
it's hard to let go
and see how
amazing you are

that's why I'm here
to keep
saying the same thing
for both of us

and together
we can let it all go
over and over
again

each time
knowing
more deeply
this message
the whole universe
is quietly yelling at us:

I love you
thank you
we're one

The Spaces in Between

I hope you have not
been paying too much attention
to my words

I hope you have
spent some time
in the spaces in between

I hope you have
fallen into the
empty gaps
and dwelt
in the silences

they are closer to the truth

I hope you have
wandered aimlessly
in the blanks
gotten lost
in the voids
surrounding
my silly attempts
at saying anything

because all these lines
are merely
a dancing around
what my heart
knows to be true

my mind's concoction
of symbols

just a bunch of fingers
pointing at the moon

ACKNOWLEDGMENTS

First and foremost, I have to thank my mother, Wes Stengel, and father, Andrew Stengel, without whom I would not exist and who have relentlessly supported me in all I do since my first breath. My biggest fear is that they will never feel the immensity of my gratitude and love for them.

After that, there is an endless list of souls who have inspired me and taught me along the way. Here is a partial one: my sister, Julia Stengel, and brother, Paul Stengel, who have unconditionally loved me and inspired me with their own creativity and courage, my soul sister Agatha Nowicki, who has always believed I can do anything and dreams bigger for me than I do for myself, Dominic Castillo, who expanded me and showed me a world beyond this one, Noelani Reynoso, who showed me what was possible by her example and willingness to guide me, Rene Miranda, who saw me as a butterfly before I burst out of my cocoon, and Michael Montondon, my creative doula.

Thank you to all my dear friends that received my poems and encouraged me to continue to share:

Kristin Cottrell, Christian Fooks, David Feinberg, James Riff, Jackie Lucero, Roxanne Armstrong, Audrey Potter, Dr. Friedemann Schaub, and so many others.

If we know each other, please know you have inspired and taught me more than you can imagine. Look closely enough at the words in this book and you will find yourself among them.

I also have to thank my editor, Sage Taylor Kingsley, who helped make this collection express more love than I thought was possible, and Stella Mongodi, whose talent, eye for beauty, and patience with me made this book more gorgeous than I could ever have imagined.

Thank you to all the Wisdom Keepers throughout time and space who have tended the fire of Truth throughout the ages so those of us groping in the darkness could eventually stumble upon it.

And lastly, thank you to Mother Earth, the greatest teacher of unconditional love!

ABOUT THE POET

Although Swava is often off exploring other magical places both on Planet Earth and beyond, and feels she belongs wherever she happens to be standing, she keeps her stuff in Pasadena, California.

In addition to writing poetry for what seems like lifetimes, she has been teaching high school English for almost 20 years. Her students have been some of her greatest teachers.

Her other passions include recognizing the mystical in every breath, standing on top of mountains at sunset, waking up to see the sunrise over the ocean, lying under the stars, sitting silently in jungles, smiling at strangers, and laughing with other humans, especially at herself.

She hopes that her poems reflect the infinite love she has discovered along the path to fully embracing her human experience and maybe also bring some love, bliss, and peace into someone else's heart.

www.ingramcontent.com/pod-product-compliance
Lightning Source LLC
LaVergne TN
LVHW05202508426
835513LV00018B/2173